Be Quiet and Pray

19 PRAYERS AND DEVOTIONALS FOR STRENGTH DURING COVID-19

Trina L. Hill

Be Quiet and Pray

DEDICATION

To everyone who continues to go through this pandemic, COVID-19. May the Lord give you peace.as He heals our land.

Be Quiet and Pray

CONTENTS

Be Quiet and Pray

ACKNOWLEDGMENTS

First, I would like to thank God for entrusting me with this assignment to write this devotional during this time. I would like to thank my husband, son, mom, and dad for supporting me during the writing process. I would also like to thank my extended family, my sister- friends, my Working Women Worship family for your prayers and support during the process.

Additionally, my special thanks to Latasha Stephens, Lynn Callaway, A'donna Garrett, Shawneda Crout, Patricia Roberson, and Carla Crawford. for helping me bring this book to life! I could not have done this without you.

1. FAITH

I know You. I have seen You do miracles before, but I am wavering. When I don't have what I feel I need, I begin to doubt You. I question if You love me. When I hear of the deaths, my faith wavers. When I hear of the illness, deaths, empty shelves, my faith wavers. Be Quiet and Pray.

Father,

I am struggling with my faith. Your word says that He that wavers is like a wave of the sea being tossed. I don't want to be tossed. I don't want to have an unstable mind, Father. I ask that You give me stability, a sound mind. I ask that You help me draw closer to You. I ask that You help me trust You. I have witnessed many miracles so I know in my mind that I can trust You yet, I struggle in my flesh. Help me to decrease in my flesh as Your Holy Spirit increases in me. Renew my mind so that I can focus on You. In Jesus' Name, Amen.

Scripture References: James 1:5-8

What can you do today to increase your Faith?

_____

_____

_____

_____

_____

_____

_____

_____

_____

_____

2. NOT ENOUGH

Today, I walked into the super store and I noticed so many empty shelves. It was unexpected ... the feeling I felt. I was taken aback. I saw people arguing about food. It reminded me of Black Friday when people fought over items. I never imagined I would see people fighting over food. In the chaos, I also noticed how people were speaking to the grocery store employees. They were shouting and speaking to them in a very disrespectful tone. I heard people shouting, "We don't have enough!" I was thinking, "Why are you buying so much? What about everyone else?" I left the store feeling confused and wanting to share my experience ... to complain. Instead, I decided to ... Be Quiet and Pray.

Father,

I ask that You provide enough and even more for Your people. Give us peace and patience with each other as we all go through this unimaginable time. Help us all operate

3

in love and compassion with one another. Your word says that the birds don't sow, reap, store away in barns and you feed them. Father, we know that we are more valuable than they are. So, help us to trust You. We know there is nothing too hard for You! Providing enough is not a large task. We love You Lord. In Jesus' Name, Amen.

Scripture References: Matthew 6:26 and Jeremiah 32:27

How has God provided for you in the past? What are you grateful for?

_____

_____

_____

_____

_____

_____

_____

_____

_____

3. MONEY

As I stood in the checkout line, I overheard a woman talking about her future. She was very concerned about the stock market, her job and her children's future. She complained about her circumstances for what felt like a lifetime, but in truth, it was only 5 minutes.

We are all guilty of the same behavior. We look at our current circumstances and we complain. The next time you want to complain about your money, stock market, or your job ...Be Quiet and Pray.

Father,

I come to You right now. I am concerned about my future. I see the stock market crashing. I see unemployment numbers rising. I am afraid. I know that Your word says for me to not worry, to be anxious for nothing. In Philippians 4:19, You said you will supply all our needs according to Your riches in glory. I trust You Lord. Help me lean on you and not what I see. Please provide every need according to Your riches. In Jesus' Name, Amen.

Scripture Reference - Philippians 4:19

Do you remember a time when you thought God wouldn't come through and He did? How did you feel?

_____

_____

_____

_____

_____

_____

_____

_____

_____

_____

_____

_____

4. MARRIAGE

It's been a long time since you have been home with your spouse all day every day! The house seems smaller and the demands on you both has increased. Who helps with homework? Who goes to the store for groceries? What happens if one of us gets sick? These questions seem to dominate discussions between the two of you. If you had issues before this trying time, the situation is now compounded, the stress and friction has increased. If you were in good standing before, you may not feel as connected. You miss the small moments of laughter or even a date night. You are pleading to know when this will end and what will we be when it does? You have your moments when you want to vent or even argue ...Be Quiet and Pray.

Father,

You know how I'm feeling. You know I've been wounded by my spouse's words. You know I long for the days when we were so in love that nothing mattered. Father, You know I miss the small moments with the two of us laughing, discussing our future or planning date night.

7

Father, Your word says in Ephesians 4 that we are to be complete humble, gentle, and patient bearing with one another in love. Give me the strength to be humble, gentle, and patient when I don't feel like it. Help me to make every effort to keep the unity of spirit in my home. I love my spouse, but I want to be closer and more connected. Make our marriage stronger. We need each other. Your word says two are better than one. Help me to see my spouse the way you see them. Let me love them the way you love me. In Jesus' Name, Amen.

Scripture References: Ephesians 4: 2-4 and Ecclesiastes 4:9-12

What are some things you love about your spouse? What are one or two things you can do to create a special moment while in quarantine?

_____

_____

_____

_____

_____

_____

_____

_____

_____

_____

5. CHILDREN

If you are a parent or caring for children, you are probably wearing multiple hats right now ...that of worker, parent, teacher, cook, etc. You are dealing with a lot of stress and every little thing they do probably irritates you. They are demanding more attention. You ask them to do something and they want to argue. You need to take action when a fight breaks out between siblings. You have had it! You want to verbally express how your children are getting on your nerves! You want to have the adult breakdown! Don't! Please! ... Be Quiet and Pray.

Father,

The children you gave me are wearing on me. I know You said that You will never put more on me than I can bear, so Father I need Your help. Remind me that my children are a blessing from You. Help me see greatness in them. Help me show them grace and mercy as we all go through this difficult time. Help me to be the parent they need right now. Let me decrease as You increase in me. Father, thank you for entrusting me with Your children and blessing my home with them. In Jesus' Name, Amen.

Scripture References: Psalms 127:3-5

How did you child/children make you smile today? What's a favorite activity you can do with them to bring joy to your home?

_____

_____

_____

_____

_____

_____

_____

_____

_____

_____

6. PARENTS

The phone rings and you hear your parents on the other end. You hear mixed emotions such as joy, worry, loneliness, peace. During this time, you see your parents as human, no longer superhuman as you did when you were a young child. You try to help them financially or make a run to the grocery store. They are ready to get out of the house. They want to spend time with friends by going back to their jobs, social clubs, volunteer events, and even church. They are in disarray because of this change at this time in their lives. Some are managing through the pain due to delayed surgeries. Others don't want to be alone. There is nothing you can do as the child, but ... Be Quiet and Pray.

Father,

I ask that You help me to honor my mother and father. Let me have patience when I speak with them. Let my words be like sweet honeycombs to their ears. Let them hear my heart and know that I will not cast them off in their old age. I will honor them in their old age. I will seek them for their wisdom because they have an understanding from a long life. Keep my parents safe and secure. Let no

11

harm come near them. Place a hedge of protection around them and keep disease and illness away from them. Bless them with a sound mind. In Jesus' Name. Amen.

Scripture References: Psalm 71:9, Job 12:12, Deuteronomy 5:16, Proverbs 23:22

What's one way you can make your parent(s) laugh today? When was the last time you told your parent(s) you appreciate them?

_____

_____

_____

_____

_____

_____

_____

_____

_____

_____

_____

7. LOSS OF LOVED ONE

She passed away last week from Coronavirus She didn't feel well and all of sudden she was in the hospital. She was my life, my role model. She taught me everything she knew and now she is gone. We can't plan a proper funeral ... no usual celebration of life. No cars. No singing. No sermon heard in the sanctuary. The entire family wasn't allowed to attend the graveside service. Be Quiet and Pray.

Father,

My loved one passed away and I didn't get to say goodbye. My heart is broken. Please help me heal from this pain. Help me to see the good in this situation. Your word says You will wipe every tear from their eyes. You said that You will heal my broken heart and bind up my wounds. Father, turn my mourning into joy. You said sorrow and mourning will disappear and I will be filled with joy and gladness. Help me experience joy and gladness. You said that You would give me perfect peace as long as my mind is stayed on You. Give me peace, Father. Help me appreciate the life lived and rejoice in knowing they are in the comfort of your arms. Heal my heart Lord. In Jesus' Name, Amen.

Scripture References: Revelation 21:4, Psalms 34:18, Psalms 147:3, Isaiah 51:11, Matthew 5:4, Isaiah 26:3

What's one way you could honor your loved one? What activity could you plan later to bring your family together to honor your loved one?

_____

_____

_____

_____

_____

_____

_____

_____

_____

_____

_____

_____

8. CONFIDENCE

The phone rings and your leader ask you to step in to lead an assignment. The meeting is in 30 minutes. You promptly go through the checklist in your mind and you immediately think you can't do this! You lead the meeting but you didn't feel it went well. Two hours later, your child asks for help on a math problem that you have no idea how to solve. You try to help and you didn't do the math correctly. You feel incompetent. You feel like you just can't do this. You are not built for this! Be Quiet and Pray.

Father,

I don't feel like I can do this. Your word says that I can do all things through You. Your word also says that I am should be strong and courageous. Father, help me to be strong and courageous.

I am struggling with my confidence. I have so many things to do and I don't have the skills for them all. I feel like I can't do this. Your word says that I am to be courageous. Help strengthen my courage. Give me the wisdom, the insight, and the confidence to do what You need me to do. Your word says that I can do all things through You. Help me to do all things in Your way … in Your will. Father, fill

15

me with boldness and confidence. Your word says that the old way has been replaced by a more glorious way. The new way gives me confidence and I can be bold. Father, help me be bold in all new things. In Jesus' Name, Amen.

Scripture References: Philippians 1:6, Philippians 4:13, Joshua 1:9, 2 Corinthians 3:11-12

When was the last time you felt confident? What did you do? How can you create that experience to remind you how you felt?

_____

_____

_____

_____

_____

_____

_____

_____

_____

_____

9. TRUST

Trusting in the Lord has been hard for you. For those that know the Lord, you may feel like you can trust Him some days, but not every day. For those who are establishing a relationship with Him, you feel lost or even alone. You thought He would come through with that new job. You were waiting on additional resources for the project. You expected Him to heal your loved one. You question whether He is real. You wonder if you can trust God. You would know His plan. Be Quiet and Pray

Father,

Your word instructs me to trust in the You with all my heart, and lean not to my own understanding but acknowledge You in all my ways. Father, I trust you today. I don't know what will happen moment by moment, but I trust You. I don't know what will happen in the days to come, but I trust You. I don't know the future, but You do. I thank you for allowing me to go through this time, drawing closer to You and trusting Your word. You said You are a God who doesn't lie. So, I trust You when You said I will never go begging for bread. I trust You when You said that You supply all my needs according to Your riches in glory. I trust You when You said by Your stripes

I am healed. I trust You when You said that all things work together for my good because I am called according to Your purpose. I trust You because you died for all of my sins and others. I trust You to heal our land. I trust You to not only restore what the canker worm stolen from me, but to give me double for the trouble. I trust You for the welfare of my family. I trust You for my children's' future. I trust You for my marriage. I trust You for every breath I take.

In Jesus' Name, Amen!

Scripture References: Proverbs 3:5-6, Philippians 4:19, Isaiah 53:5, Joel 2:25, Romans 8:28

When was the last time you took a leap of faith by doing something you were afraid to do? How did you feel afterwards?

_____

_____

_____

_____

_____

_____

_____

_____

10. EXHAUSTION

It's several weeks in and you are exhausted. You feel like you're doing everything for everybody. You have full days; meetings at work, teaching classes, cooking three meals a day, cleaning, washing, and so much more! You shop for your family and others several times a week. You check in on neighbors and family members. You are tired, mentally exhausted. You wonder when it will all end. You see family members relaxed and happy. On the inside, you're angry because they don't understand you are exhausted! Can't they see it ... Be Quiet and Pray.

Father,

I am exhausted! I feel like I am carrying the entire load! I need a moment to myself. Your word says to come to You when I'm carrying a heavy load and You will give me rest. Father, give me rest. I am leaning on You Lord. Your word says don't grow weary in well doing. Help me to remember this as I care for others. Give me what I need to do what You have called me to do. In Jesus' Name, Amen.

Scripture References: Matthew 11:28-30, Isaiah 40:31, Galatians 6:9-10

What are 3 things you are willing to do to take better care of yourself?

_____

_____

_____

_____

_____

_____

_____

_____

_____

_____

_____

_____

_____

_____

_____

_____

11. LONELINESS

You walked into the house and it is completely silent. There isn't another person there. You feel so alone. You turn on the TV or radio but that doesn't take away the lonely feeling. You pick up a book or work on a long overdue project to overcome that lonely feeling but that doesn't fill the lonely space. You call friends and family, but they don't understand your feeling because they aren't experiencing loneliness. During the day, things are okay, but at night when you would usually be out with friends or exploring your city, now you are stuck at home. It is difficult to erase your lonely feeling ... Be Quiet and Pray.

Father,
Your word said You are all I need. Holy Spirit help me to be content. Your word in Matthew says you are always with me to the end of the age. Your word is what I'll trust and believe. In Jesus' Name, Amen.

Scripture References - Matthew 28:19-20

When you feel alone, write down two things you can do or two people you can call.

21

Be Quiet and Pray

_____

_____

_____

_____

_____

_____

_____

_____

_____

_____

_____

_____

_____

_____

_____

_____

_____

_____

12. LEADERSHIP

Every day you are bombarded with messages from our local or national leaders. In addition to those messages, you are also inundated by communications from leaders in your company and possibly schools. You don't understand why they are making the decisions they are making. They can't see what you see ... know what you know. It's frustrating. You end your day venting about how terrible they are and how you can do things better. It's natural ... it's your nature.

The next time, you start to say something about our leaders ... Be Quiet and Pray.

Father,

You know I am beyond frustrated. I don't like what my government officials and other leaders are doing or saying. I don't agree with their decisions. I don't understand. Your word says in Timothy that we are to pray for our leaders that they may live peaceful and quiet lives in all godliness and holiness. I pray for every leader in every organization across the world will seek You and Your strength. Give them wisdom to humble themselves and listen to Godly counsel. Soften their hearts and open their ears. Do not let the spirit of pride overtake them. Strengthen them where they may be weak. I pray that they make the right decisions, as it relates to Your people. In Jesus' Name, Amen.

Scripture References: 1 Timothy 2 1-2, Chronicles 16:11

Can you identify 3 things that your leaders did to help you, your company, or your community?

_____

_____

_____

_____

_____

_____

_____

_____

_____

_____

13. LEADING AT WORK

You join the call and instead of hearing the voices of the team, you hear children screaming in the background, dogs barking, and a door bell ringing! You wonder if you are on a work call or if you are talking to a friend who is home for the holidays. You notice the tension in one of your employee's faces. You notice one is missing, while some are disengaged. When one of the employees speaks, you see disgust on the face of another employee. You wonder why we are treating each other like this especially during these times. Businesses are constantly changing and some on the team struggle with change. Stress and anxiety are high! How can you lead them during this time? What can you do to help them focus on execution while you focus on helping them remove roadblocks? You wonder what do they need and are you the one for the job ... Be Quiet and Pray.

Father,

I come to You asking You to instruct me and teach me the way I should go. You said in your word that You would counsel me with your loving eye on me. Please teach me and counsel me. You said that great kings give countries stability. Help me provide stability, peace, and guidance to my people. Help me be what You need me to be for them during this time. Help me model Your love, mercy, and grace as I provide instruction. Let the words out of my mouth and the meditation of my heart be acceptable in your sight. Your word says that if I am lacking wisdom and I ask you, You will give it generously. Father, give me an abundance of wisdom so that I may provide what my team needs, what my company needs, and what my people need. In Jesus' Name, Amen.

Scripture References: Psalms 32:8, Psalms 19:14, Proverbs 29:4

Who do you confide in? Do you know two or three people who have led through similar times and seek their counsel?

_____

_____

_____

_____

_____

_____

_____

_____

14. THOSE WHO HATE YOU

Why are they attacking me right now? Why are they slandering my name? I'm trying to get my work done for the company. I'm trying to take care of my people, my patients, my customers, and my family. Why are they attacking me again? When will this end? Why are they yelling at me? Why are they refusing to do their work? Why don't they answer when I email or call them? What did I do to deserve this treatment?

People seem to go after you more during stressful times. Sometimes it's not you, it's them. It doesn't feel good, but remember, you never know what is going on behind closed doors.

Be encouraged ... Be Quiet and Pray.

Father,

I come to You humbling myself before You, asking You to help me to love those that hate me as You love. It is hard to experience attacks during this time. It is hard to love those who attack me or who put my livelihood at risk. You said that my faith is forced into the open when I am under pressure. You also said that I am to do the work so that I mature. It is hard Lord. My flesh wants to fight back, but my spirit says to obey Your word. You said that I am to pray for those who despitefully use me. It is hard so help me. Help me see them as you see them. Bless them and their families. In Jesus' Name. Amen.

Scripture References: Luke 6:27-28, Matthew 5:44, James 1:3-6

How can you kill those that hate you with kindness? What can you do to be more patient with them?

_____

_____

_____

_____

_____

_____

_____

Be Quiet and Pray

_____

_____

_____

_____

_____

_____

_____

_____

_____

_____

_____

_____

_____

15. OVERWHELMED

I can't breathe. I feel my heart racing. My chest is tight. I can't breathe. I am trying to care for the sick, but I can't breathe. I feel overwhelmed. I don't know what to do. Be Quiet and Pray.

Father,

Your word said that I should fear not, for You are with me. I am afraid. I see so much and so much is asked of me. Help me to take a breath. Give me the strength to do what You have called me to do. Help me to take care of the sick. Your word says when I have done unto the least of these, I have done unto You. Father, help me to care for them like You care for me. When I start to feel panicky, out of breath, help me to remember to simply breathe. You breathed life into me. Help me to inhale You, Father! Send the Holy Spirit to minister to me. In Jesus' Name, Amen.

Scripture References: Matthew 24:40, Genesis 2:7

When you begin to feel overwhelmed, what's one thing you can focus on that brings you solace or makes you laugh?

Be Quiet and Pray

31

16. GOD, I'M ANGRY!

I am angry with You, with people, with the government, with every one! I miss my parents, kids can't attend prom, graduation. You all have taken everything from me, my job, and my time with time with my family, my health. Several churches and schools are closed. Plans for vacation and family reunions were cancelled. Why did you do this? I don't know what to do with this anger....Be Quiet and Pray.

Father,

I am sad. I am angry. Help me to see things the way You see them. Help me to understand. I know that You don't operate the way I do. I am angry with the situation. You said that I am to be quick to listen, slow to speak and slow to anger. I know that human anger doesn't produce righteousness. Heal the hurt and the pain which shows up in my anger. Help me show mercy to others as you shown mercy toward me. In Jesus' Name. Amen.

Scripture References: James 1:19-20, Psalms 10:1, Lamentations 5:20 & Jeremiah 12:1

When you start to feel angry with God, what is the root of your anger? Is it that you don't have control?

_____

_____

_____

_____

_____

_____

_____

_____

_____

_____

_____

_____

_____

_____

_____

17. PEACE

We are all home at the same time, working online. There are 3 digital learning sessions and there are 2 Zoom corporate meetings going on. The dogs are barking while two cellphones are ringing! My children are asking me a to teach them the way their teacher teaches, and I am clueless. The house seemed larger before this happened, but no longer. There is nowhere I can go to have peace. Have a moment of silence. I can't hear my self-think. We just ran out of toilet tissue!....Be Quiet and Pray

Father,

I come to you begging that You give me peace that surpasses all understanding. My home, my life right now is chaotic. I can't find a corner anywhere where I can just find peace. When Jesus' was in the midst of the storm, he said "Peace be still." Give me that power so that I can speak peace and it comes. Help me to speak over chaos and remain in peace throughout the day. Thank you in advance for peace. In Jesus' Name, Amen.

Scripture References: Philippians 4:7, John 14:27

When was the last time you felt at peace? What were you
doing? Can you recreate that experience?

_____

_____

_____

_____

_____

_____

_____

_____

_____

_____

_____

_____

_____

_____

_____

_____

18. TIMING

The hours are turning into days. Days turning into weeks, and now weeks into months. Seems that you can no longer keep track of the days. You feel like you can't stay home much longer. You're ready to get out of the house. It's time to go back to work, back to your old way of life. You don't' understand why the pandemic isn't over yet.

God's timing is not our timing. His ways are not our ways ... Be Quiet and Pray.

Father,

Help me to submit to Your will. Help me to move when You want me to move versus when I feel like moving. Help me to surrender my need to do what I think is important for what is really important. Lord, help me to focus on what I need, which is You. In Your word, You reminded Martha that she was worried about many things but she only needed You. Lord, let me be like Mary. Mary sat at Your feet and listened. Let me see this time as a precious opportunity to sit with You without the distractions of life. In Jesus' Name, Amen.

Scripture References: Luke 10:38-42

In the past, was there a time when you wanted something instantly, but God required you to wait? Was it worth the wait?

_____

_____

_____

_____

_____

_____

_____

_____

_____

_____

_____

_____

_____

_____

_____

19. NEW NORMAL – NEW THING

The impact of COVID-19 has altered our lives. So many things are changing around us. Students at all levels have encountered online education. Will that remain the same? Will the traditional brick and mortar school become extinct? Churches are now leveraging digital platforms. Will they go back to a traditional church setting? Are we equipped for the future? What skills will we need for the future to navigate in the new normal? How will we emerge? ... Be Quiet and Pray.

Father,

Your word says that we are to forget the things that are behind and press forward to the things that are ahead. Help me see what is in front of me. Teach me the right skills needed for the future. Your word says that a righteous man/woman's steps are ordered by the Lord. Order my steps. This is a new path and I don't know what to do. I don't know how to plan for my future. You know Father. You know my comings and my goings. You know my beginning and my ending. You knew me when you knitted me in my mother's womb. Help me to see Your vision for my new life. Help me to mourn the past, press forward, and move toward what You have for me. Equip me for the work that is ahead. Help me to identify my gifts and talents that will serve You during this time. I know You are doing a new thing! I can't wait to see it. In Jesus' Name, Amen.

Scripture References: Psalms 139:13, Philippians 3:13, Isaiah 43:19

What is God birthing in you? What are you doing for His glory during this season? What are you looking forward to?

_____

_____

_____

_____

_____

_____

_____

_____

_____

_____

_____

_____

ABOUT THE AUTHOR

Trina L. Hill is an author, technology leader, speaker, coach, and woman of faith. For over twenty years, Trina, has motivated, inspired, and coached individuals to see themselves beyond the professional and personal seat they occupy.

Connect with Trina on her website at
www.trinalhill.com

Made in the USA
San Bernardino, CA
03 August 2020